CADDY TALES

G000123796

Introduction

Chapter 1   Wrong Ball

Chapter 2   Five Iron

Chapter 3   Birthday Present

Chapter 4   Air Wolf

Chapter 5   The Magical Round

Chapter 6   Caddie Training Sir!

Chapter 7   Largest Tip Ever

Chapter 8   Caddie Nicknames

Chapter 9   Member / Guest

Chapter 10   Unforgettable Quotes

FOREWORD

If there is one thing we can learn from "Frank the Tank", it's spend time at a party with the guy who has a nickname. Scott, "The Squirrel" Werner is one of those guys. If you are lucky enough to spend more than five minutes with the man, you will undoubtedly find yourself in a laughing state. He is crazy like a fox, borderline insane, yet at times a complete genius. The life of any party "The Squirrel" has more stories about the golfing world then any PGA Pro, player, caddie, or casual fan. The events that have taken place in his life are both hilarious and completely unbelievable. A cross between a kid in the candy store and your financial planner, Scotty's passion for storytelling and making people laugh is clearly evident in his work.

It has been interesting to say this least, working with Scott on this book. At times I have laughed, been frustrated, and on several occasions been in complete shock after hearing some of his stories. People have always told 'The Squirrel" that he should write a book and fill it with all of these crazy golf course events. Finally, Scotty said, "why the heck not", and thus you now hold in your hands the end result.

Be forewarned, Caddy Tales doesn't read like a college textbook or any normal book in fact. It has some crazy sentence structure and reads just as if someone were telling you what happened to them last weekend; that is the complete intent of the book. The goal of the book is not to take you to some fictional world or epic atmosphere; it's to make you feel like you are with your buddies or playing nine holes with your weekly golf league and one of your friends is telling you a story about something crazy that happened to them. Expect to relax and hear a few funny stories about what really happens on the golf course from the perspective of the "man on the bag". So try to image you are with a group of friends on the golf course, or hanging around the water cooler and someone says, "Hey do I have a story for you". Sit back, relax and enjoy reading Caddy Tales.

-Matthew M. Bakowicz, PGA

INTRODUCTION

Caddy Tales is a collection of stories from the viewpoint of a caddie. These stories take place in many of the golf courses around the world. I have had the privilege of caddying for celebrities, millionaires, billionaires, sports legends, and individuals who were the salt of the earth. The stories told in this book are in no way intended to make fun of anyone. Members and guests have shared these stories on numerous occasions in the club house, after the round, or even on the golf course the next day. I thought it might bring a smile to a readers face if they knew what went on while a caddie is working for such unique individuals. So sit back and enjoy the literary journey we are about to take together.

WRONG BALL SIR

Early in the mornings at any private golf course there is always a combination of commotion and confusion. The operators on the mowers are furiously attempting to finish mowing the greens, fairways and tees, and the practice range. The outside service staff is hastily setting up the range stations before the early golfers arrive for their practice sessions. The golf staff discusses a multitude of morning details with respect to pairings, order of play, guest play, and where to meet at the end of the day for cocktails.

The caddies assemble in the caddie shack and await there loop assignments. In caddie lingo a loop is either a nine or eighteen hole task of carrying a golf bag for a member or guest. After which, you are hoping to get paid handsomely. Some of the caddies wait patiently; others sleep, drink gallons of coffee, tell amusing stories of the previous night's escapades, or whine incessantly about things that nobody cares about.

On this particular morning I was lucky enough to be assigned a loop for a two ball. A two ball is two members, or any two players that are going to either play nine or eighteen holes. Most caddies prefer two balls because the loop is usually much quicker than a four ball and since they are carrying two bags they are maximizing their cash earnings.

I walked out to the range to greet my players and start my day. On this morning I had Mr. Wiggins and his guest, Mr. Napa. Now you may be thinking that this guy owns half of Napa Valley Wine Country, which would be a good thing for all of us, but he does not. Mr. Napa was a financial advisor who advised Mr. Wiggins. Apparently, if you have more money than you can count, you require a guy who can tell you what to buy, sell or save. I personally think that if you have that kind of money, what the hell do you need a guy like this for; but that's just my opinion.

My two players finished warming up and we headed to the first tee. Mr. Napa had never played the course previously, so I knew he might need some extra assistance. I told him that if he had any questions, to simply ask and I would help. The gentlemen teed off and we began our walk down the fairway.

It was an early morning, approximately 6:45 am, and as we walked down the fairway the sun was just coming over the trees. It was pleasant with the temperature around 70 degrees. The sun bounced off the wet fescue and it looked like there were thousands of tiny diamonds hanging all around the golf course.

The first hole, a par 4, is a little bit of a challenge since it is approximately 454 yards and it is a dog leg to the right. You really need to hit a long tee shot in order to have a chance to get to the green in regulation. And in case you try to cut the corner, there are three menacing bunkers just waiting there to gobble up your golf ball. My two players did not play this hole badly; however, they each finished with a double bogey, a 6. As we made our way to the second hole, Mr. Napa commented on how beautiful the course was and since it was still before 7, the maintenance staff was still finishing up a little work on the front nine and I mentioned to him that is would look even better as soon as the maintenance crew had finished there work.

As I approached the green it was my surprise to see that each player had a birdie putt. The reason that this surprised me was because this green had many undulations and was protected by a diabolical bunker in front. If that is not enough, it even had a false front that will break your ankle. When you're on this green both you and your caddie need to pay particular attention to the bunker on the front of the green. Sometimes, if the flag is near the bunker, and your putt is too firm, it has a tendency to hop right in. This morning, that became a reality for Mr. Wiggins. He hit the putt with a little bit too much pace and it began to race by the hole toward the bunker. Now, some players like to talk to their golf ball. They ask it to go, sit, get down, turn, fade, and sometimes many other things that are not appropriate for this story.

As it went past the hole it seemed like this golf ball had a chance to wind up in the bunker. Mr. Wiggins began trying to talk the ball out of the bunker. Well after a second or two, it was very clear that the ball was going to wind up in the sand and unless a miracle was to occur, nothing was going to stop it. Mr. Napa and I realized this; however, Mr. Wiggins did not. He gave it the old college try. He told it to sit then he told it to stop. His pleading got desperate as he began to beg. "Oh God please don't go into the bunker, for the love of God, no, no, no.!"

"It was such a good putt, please stop on the fringe, please, please, please. " I looked at Mr. Napa and he just smiled back at me and shrugged his shoulders. A second later, the ball went into the bunker and the world came to an end.

Mr. Wiggins putter went flying through the air like a javelin at a decathlon. Ok, it was more like a dart you throw at the county fair to pop a balloon and win a stuffed squirrel, but you get the picture. He danced around the green for what seemed to be an eternity. Mr. Napa said this happens once in a while so we just let him get it out of his system. While he was twirling around the green like a top, we watched Dave, one of the maintenance workers, on the sprayer drive down the fifth fairway. Mr. Napa asked me what the white dots were that seemed to be leaking out of the sprayer. I told him it was soap suds. See when they spray, the material that they put down does not have any color. So when they turn around to spray the other side of the fairway, the soap suds make a little line so they don't overlap where they just were. Then after about an hour, the suds disappear. He thought that was cool.

We played number three, but relived number two. Mr. Wiggins thought that the golf gods singled him out on the last hole and he believed that he was the only one in the world it has ever happened to. I tried to reassure him that it happens to more people than you think. We completed the hole and number two became a distant memory.

Number four is a vicious par 3. I think it is one of the hardest holes on the golf course. Out of bounds lies off to the right and a false front that rivals any top notch front that you might see on TV. Bunkers guard the entire left side and the fescue around the hole is waist high. Other than that, it's easy. On this particular morning the flag was in the back left corner of the green. Although it's a difficult hole, this pin location lends itself to a possible hole in one. Provided: you gauge the wind, pick the right club, line your tee shot up correctly, hit the shot perfectly, land it on the green within a specific 4 inch circle, and get a little bit of luck. Well, Mr. Napa did everything correctly, except he needed a little more luck. The ball sailed off of his hybrid club and made a beeline for the back right part of the green. Once it hit the green it started on its journey to the hole. A few hills later it stopped right next to the hole; an easy birdie.

Mr. Wiggins hit a similar shot, however it ran out of steam on the way to the hole and finished on the top of the ridge about 20 feet from the hole. An impossible putt to get close to the hole, it was as if he was putting on a table top. He tried to make the putt to tie the hole, but it sailed past with a vengeance. As the ball went past the hole it received a tongue lashing similar to the putt on the second hole.

We stood on the fifth tee and took some time to savor the moment. We were the only ones on the golf course, and it looked spectacular. The sun was low in the sky and it was extremely peaceful. This par 5 stretched out over the links style front nine to the tune of 550 yards. On the right was a huge waste bunker that seemed to invite any player that hit a fade. On the left side were a series of bunkers and some fescue that once visited turned the hole into a par 6 immediately. Mr. Napa, he hit his right down the middle.

However, halfway there Mother Nature had a little bit of influence on where this ball was going to wind up. A gentle breeze pushed the ball from left to right. Along with the breeze the ball seemed to fade a little bit. The end result caused the ball to end up in the light rough on the right just short of the waste bunker.

Next to tee off was Mr. Wiggins. Driving was not his strong suit, but on this day I believe he swung the club with a little anger that might have been in his body from the unfortunate results on number two and number four. This ball rocketed off his clubface and went right through the wind. It was as straight as an arrow and landed in the fairway just short of Mr. Napa's ball. I began walking towards Mr. Wiggin's ball and he flew past me like a cheetah chasing dinner. It was probably more like a turtle passing a snail, but you get the picture. Mr. Napa veered off to the right and I told him I would be with him in just a minute as soon as I gave Mr. Wiggins his yardage and a club. As I arrived next to Mr. Wiggins, he immediately asked me for a yardage. I started to tell him, "Mr. Wiggins, you don't want the yardage from here, this................." He quickly cut me off. "Scotty, when I ask for a yardage, I expect that you would give it to me. I don't want an excuse. If you don't have the yardage, that's ok. Take your time and get me the yardage." I paused for a moment. I'm used to dealing with different personalities and challenging situations, so I took a second for myself before responding. Once again I said "Mr. Wiggins this yardage is not going to help you because......................" again I was interrupted. "Scotty you have been here long enough to know not to give me an excuse. I want you to tell me the yardage because I have to make up my mind whether to hit the 3 wood from here or hit the 5 wood. Now, for the last time, what is my yardage from here?" I bit my tongue and said, "You have 319 yards from here". He took his three wood and I made my way over to the other player. Mr. Napa inquired, "What was going on over there?" I replied, "Just watch and you will have a story to tell your friends for the rest of your life."

Mr. Wiggins took a few practice swings and stepped right up to the ball. He took a deep breath and lined his shot up with the middle of the fairway. He took the club back slowly and when he reached the top of his backswing, he came down with enough club head speed to hit this ball to another planet.

Unfortunately, he was not hitting his ball. He had stopped next to a perfectly round ball of foam that was dropped on the fairway from the sprayer. Now as you may have already guessed, I was trying to tell him that his ball was about 8 yards farther down the fairway and that he was standing next to a perfectly round ball of foam that looked like his golf ball. But as you now know, he would have none of that conversation, and BAM... here comes Karma.

When the three wood first came into contact with the ball of foam it was a sight I will never forget, neither will Mr. Napa. The ball of foam exploded into a trillion pieces. For a brief second it looked as if there were thousands of stars dotting the skies. Then as the small stars of foam gently fell back to earth, so did Mr. Wiggins. When there was no resistance to stop the golf club (because there was no golf ball), his momentum helped him perform moves that would have landed him a job at Cirque Du Soleil. I think he spun around three times before he hit the ground and lay there like a 9 year old making a snow angel.

The silence was broken by the laughter of Mr. Napa. He laughed so hard he could not finish the hole. Tears were streaming down his face and he was holding his belly like a prize fighter just hit him. He was trying to tell us how funny he thought it was but he was laughing so hard he made no sense whatsoever. We finished the round and we said our goodbyes. As a caddie you always want to make sure the member or guest has a great experience. And sometimes you just have to let people be, or else you won't have a story to tell.

FIVE IRON

It was an early February morning, and the driving range was full of players. My manager introduced me to my players, and I was overcome with a tremendous feeling that can be summed up with this simple sentence; "Oh what a story lies going to be a very interesting day. Now first let me set the scene for you by explaining that when a caddie is working for a group that is gambling, the tips always have the potential of becoming huge. Let me break down the game these four players were involved in. The two teams were John and Dougie vs. Tony and Matt. They all worked for the same company and each year they met in Orlando for a sales convention. During the convention they would get away to play a match. The format of this game was going to be a 2 person best ball and the stakes were 100 bucks a hole. If the hole is tied, then the money carries over to the next hole. So if three holes were tied in a row, the following hole would be worth 400 bucks. And, just to throw a little icing on the cake, if anyone wins with a birdie on the hole, the money doubles.

When the stakes become large, the group tends to spend a little extra time on the first tee box going over some rules so there is no controversy as the match continues. They went over the standard rules: 1 ball off the first tee, putt the ball in the hole, no "gimme's", and the last one in which they spent what seemed an eternity on was, play the ball down no matter where it lies. Before we continue, let me tell you how this conversation went. John said to Matt, "every time we play down here in Florida, you bend over and touch the ball and gently roll it over to make sure it is yours. After you make sure it's yours, it always seems to be sitting up perfectly in the rough, or wherever it is that you looked at it. So today, we play the ball down no matter where it is! I mean no touching the ball whatsoever until it is on the green! Are we all in agreement to this rule?" All of the players agreed that today we would play the ball down. John was very adamant about this rule and it was evident by the color of his face after the discussion, it was as red as a ripe tomato in July.

Then, as we approached the end of the negotiations, they started to talk about handicaps. This is an adjustment given to players in order to make the game "more fair". They decided that John and Tony would play even, and Dougie and Matt would each get 4 strokes from the other players. This basically means that on the four hardest holes on the golf course, Dougie and Matt get to reduce there actual score by 1 stroke. Now we were ready to play some golf!

If any of you out there have ever played in a Club Championship, or a Member / Member tournament or even tried to qualify for your Players Ability Test (PAT) you know that the tension on the first tee box is unbelievable. I have caddied for millionaires, billionaires and as Forrest Gump would say, GOZILLIONAIRES, and it is always the same on the first tee box. Which of course reminds me of the classic saying; you could cut the tension with a knife.

The first hole was somewhat lackluster and the hole was tied with two pars. So this meant that the second hole was worth 200 bucks. As the players teed off on number 2, John's tee shot went further left than Nancy Pelosi. At this particular time, Tony reminded John of the rule, play your ball down, no touching it or moving it around to identify it. The group got a small chuckle out of this. I found John's ball, but it was of no help whatsoever. He was behind a bush and had to punch out to the fairway. I thought it was almost impossible to get the ball back into the fairway because he had another branch behind him that was going to impede his swing. I tried to tell him this in a somewhat nice manner, but he would have none of it. He took a swing at the ball and the only thing that went out into the fairway was the pine straw. About 3 seconds later his club was in the fairway after a few poignant expletives. I was laughing......... on the inside. This hole turned out to be what we caddies call a "snowball fight". Let me explain. In the golf industry, if you have a terrible hole and you score an 8, we usually call that *Frosty the Snowman.* It gets its name because of the way it is written on the score card. On the card it looks like the base of a snowman you may have built when we were little. Hence a snowball fight means that everyone is having a terrible hole and it's probably going to be a tie with a couple of 8's. This hole lived up to that standard. John was hitting out of the bushes, Dougie hit his in the water......twice, Tony plugged it in the bunker, and Matt hit his so far over the green that it was in another state. So after what seemed to take an hour, Dougie and Tony tied the hole with, you guessed it…………..8's.

A hole like this is actually good for the group. They relax a little bit and the tension seems to ease from their swings and they play a little better. This was evident on the third hole as John hit an iron shot to within 12 feet. It looked like they were going to win the hole because in order to tie the hole, Matt was going to have to make a 40 foot putt. Now, this is where I get a chance to earn my money as a caddie. Matt asked me to read the putt for him, and it was one that I have seen many times before. Now at this particular course the reason I am so good on the greens is because I have seen the putts hundreds and hundreds of times. I am a good green reader, but not quite as good as my fellow caddies and friends at Pinehurst and Pebble Beach. I pointed to a spot for Matt to roll his ball over. I was confident that if he hit this spot, gravity would take over and the ball would funnel right to the hole. Matt hit the spot dead solid perfect and the roller coaster ride began. It ended by hitting the back of the cup, popping up like a gopher coming out of a hole, then disappeared below the rim. A series of chest bumps and high fives ensued. John now had to make his 12 foot putt to tie the hole instead of winning. Sometimes when the other team makes a putt like this, it tends to make the hole look a little smaller for the next person to putt. John took his time and jarred the putt. This is where the story gets good!

The next hole was now worth 400 bucks. The hole was pretty much a straight forward par 4. It was 395 yards with a large fairway. There was a lateral hazard on both sides of the fairway, but you really had to hit an errant shot to reach either one. The cart path for the hole extended down the right side and the green was about 45 yards deep with the flag in the back. John was first to tee off and he hit a bullet down the left hand side of the fairway. It came to rest just short of the 150 yard marker. Dougie then launched one down the middle and this laser beam never left the center of the fairway. Matt was next, hitting an absolute bomb down the right side of the fairway about 310 yards. Tony was the final player to hit, and unfortunately, he came over the top a little bit and hit a slice down the right side of the fairway.

It bounced in the rough, took a squirrelly kick to the right and landed smack in the middle of the cart path. All of the players went to their respective golf balls and I stayed with Tony since he was actually the farthest from the hole. When he came up and looked at where his golf ball was we started discussing options since his ball was on the cart path. As we were talking, from out of nowhere John flew over in his golf cart like Jimmy Johnson finishing the Daytona 500. John asked what we were talking about and Tony told him we were discussing where to drop his golf ball since it was in the middle of the cart path.

He mentioned that I told him we could drop it on either side, as long as it was no closer to the hole. John proceeds to go on a tirade. First he told me to shut up and stated, "Scotty you stay out of this, we have a big money match and you should not pretend to be a rules official." Tony came to my defense, but John was so fired up, it went in one ear and out the other. John reminded Tony "at the beginning of the match we said we were playing the ball down no matter where it was!" All of the players started arguing and said it was implied that you should always get a drop off of a cement cart path. John screamed at the top of his lungs "we said we are playing the ball down, and we are playing the ball down! No touching, no rolling, no drops. You play the ball as it lies today." It was and understatement to say John was making the entire group uncomfortable.

Tony was now angrier than John. He looked at me and said "Scotty, what is my yardage?" With my voice cracking, I told him it was 156 yards to the middle of the green and the flag was plus 16. So the yardage to the hole was 172 yards. Tony took out a club and looked directly at John and said, "Can I take a practice swing?" John said you can do whatever the hell you want, just don't move the ball. Tony stepped up and took a violent practice swing! The club skidded off of the cement and it looked like the 4th of July. He turned to John and asked again, "Can I take another one?" John just nodded his head. At this point in time you could feel that the entire group was uneasy. The golf match was no longer fun. I thought it was going to be a WWE cage match here on the fairway. Tony took another swing and more sparks flew from the club and the cement. I could not believe my eyes. The fairway almost caught on fire because of the sparks. Just what we need in Florida, another brush fire caused by an angry golfer.

Tony settled down and lined up his shot. You could have heard a pin drop it was so quiet. Tony took a swipe at the ball and once the club hit the cement again it looked like he launched a roman candle. This ball took off like a missile and never left the flag stick. It hit in the middle of the green and rolled up to the cup stopping only 4 inches away! It was an amazing shot. Matt came over and gave Tony a high five as Dougie just shook his head and John just stared at his own feet. John finally came over to Tony and congratulated him on the shot. John said, "See, all that crying about playing the golf ball down and you hit a shot like that. The hole is worth 400 bucks and birdies pay double. So you guys are going to probably win 800 because of that shot. You should be happy we are playing the ball down. By the way what did you hit?

Tony paused for a second and said "I hit your 5 iron!" In all the commotion, Tony went over to John's bag and took out his 5 iron. By the time he was finished with the practice swings, the bottom of the club looked like it went through a meat grinder. As Tony walked back to his cart, he tossed the mangled 5 iron back to John and said "Karma is a bitch, aint it?"

BIRTHDAY PRESENT

Ladies events are extremely fun, and caddying for them always results in a great story. Let me take you back to a ladies member guest event. It was a Monday in late January. The event usually starts around 9:00 am and after the round of golf, the ladies have lunch and talk about their game.

During this particular morning, the outside staff was dressed in light blue shirts and greeted all of the players as they arrived. The spectacle of vehicles that arrived was quite impressive. Since this was an ultra-private golf course in Florida, we had Bentley's, Rolls Royce's, Tesla's and every color Ferrari you could possibly imagine.

As the ladies walked to the driving range to warm up and hit a few shots, all of the caddies followed to join their group. We all introduced ourselves and starting cleaning the clubs and in general, talking with our players in order to get to know them. Since we were walking today, each caddie would carry 2 bags. My foursome included the two ladies I was carrying for Mrs. Pravda and Mrs. White and the other caddie in the foursome, Mike, had Mrs. Trudeux and Mrs. Little.

In an event of this size the golf staff usually assigns each group a starting hole, instead of having tee times. By doing this, all of the teams can start and finish at the same time. In the golf industry we call this a shotgun. Our group was going to start on hole number 2. This means after we played the 18th hole we will still have to go back and play number 1. This ensures that all the players finish at approximately the same time. Mike and I started to walk to the second hole to try and arrive before our players. The golf staff would ride our members and their guest out to hole number two just a few moments before 9'o clock.

Once all of the players were dropped off, the tournament would start with the blowing of a loud horn. The horn pierced the morning air and the tournament began.

Now when you are carrying a player's bag you are usually privy to a few juicy conversations and this morning was no different. Immediately after teeing off Mrs. Pravda asked if there was a rest room close by. We proceeded to let her know that there was one after we teed off on number four. Mrs. White asked her why she had to go to the bathroom already and she proceeded to tell the group what she had for dinner last night. Evidently Mrs. Pravda was at a fancy dinner the evening before and all of the food was too delicious to pass up. She had: lobsters with drawn butter, little crab cake appetizers (not as good as my moms, a Maryland native), herb infused filet mignon, (a specialty of Chef Kevin), pigs in a blanket, twice baked potatoes, Cesar salad, shrimp cocktail, scrumptious breads, and a selection of meat and cheeses that were to die for. Then when the dessert tray arrived she tried just a little sample of each one. After hearing what she had to eat for dinner it was amazing to think she had room for more. But the dessert sampling consisted of tiny chocolate chip cookies, three different kinds of ice cream, (she said she only had a scoop of each), and cheese cake. I have no idea how she fit all of this into her tiny belly. After all, Mrs. Pravda was only about 5 foot 2 inches tall and tipped the scales at a whopping 100 pounds. However, it seemed like this dinner put her at about 110 and her body was now making attempts to return her to that 100 pound figure that she enjoyed so much.

The other ladies were amazed by the amount of calories she consumed. Mrs. Pravda said that she could wait until we reached number 4, which would allow her to then do number 2. As we played, Mrs. Trudeux asked what the occasion was for last night's party in which she consumed enough calories to support a tri-athlete for a week. She proceeded to tell the group that it was a birthday party for her and she invited about 125 of her closest friends. I don't even have 125 friends on *Facebook*!

One of the gifts that she received was a pair of golf gloves. Now these were not just regular gloves they were monogrammed golf gloves. Stenciled on each glove in pure Italian silk were her three initials. She was very proud of this gift and she was happy enough to talk about it for the rest of the day. I could tell you about the other gifts she received, but there is no way in the world you would believe me, so I will leave them to your imagination.

As we finished the third hole you could see the

joy in Mrs. Pravda's face as she saw the bathrooms were only a 9 iron away. After all of the ladies hit their tee shots they went to use the rest rooms. Mike and I walked down the fairway and positioned the bags by the player's golf balls and patiently waited. As you could well imagine we had to wait a few extra minutes for Mrs. Pravda. This was understandable, it happens to all of us at one time or another. Well she came bouncing out of the bathroom and skipped down the fairway like she was in a Disney movie. She was smiling from ear to ear and boy she was ready to play golf. She gave me a paper towel that she had used to dry her hands and politely asked me if I could throw it out. I said certainly, and put it in my bib. There are trash cans on most holes, so this was no problem at all. When we arrived at the next tee box I went to throw the paper towel away. Since the trash can was behind me Mike bet me one dollar that I could not make it into the trash can from 10 feet away. Well I took the bet. As you may or may not know, caddies bet on everything! And when I mean everything, I mean everything. We bet on the first player to curse, which member will pee in the woods the most number of times, who gets blamed for a bad read on a putt, first player to throw a club, you get the picture. You name it, we bet on it.

Well, I took my time, thought about the distance, factored in the wind and let the paper towel fly. Well I lost; it hit the top and bounced out. I hate losing. I went over to retrieve the paper towel and throw it away. As I did, I noticed Mrs. Pravda's golf glove was wrapped up in the towel. I threw the paper towel away and hooked her golf glove back to the handle of her golf bag. Some players keep their glove in their back pocket and some keep it wrapped around their bag. I asked Mike for a chance to win my dollar back. He said ok and we would certainly find something else to bet on during the rest of the round. We always do.

As we got deeper into the tournament, the day started to heat up as well. Not only was it a little hot, but the humidity was rising also. This makes it a little challenging to grip the golf club. We were coming up to a very long par 4 and the ladies prepared to hit their shots. The first three ladies piped their drives down the fairway. Mrs. Pravda was last to tee off. As the humidity climbed, she found it hard to grip the club. She came over to her bag to get one of her monogrammed gloves and took the one that was hooked to the handle. She put the glove on, bent over to tee the ball up and all hell broke loose!

She started screaming hysterically like someone was pulling off her fingernails one at a time. She was leaping off of the ground like she was on a pogo stick. The lady was going totally berserk. The screams were deafening and she began to shake her hand violently like it was on fire. We all watched in absolute disbelief. What in the hell was going on? Nothing she was saying was making sense; it was a bunch of high pitched screams. Finally after what seemed like an eternity she had taken off her golf glove and threw it to the ground. Then, as if the golf glove was possessed, she started beating it with her driver. She was hitting it like it had a life of its own and she needed to end its life right here on this tee box. When there was no life left in the glove and Mrs. Pravda was out of energy we finally got the real story. The five of us could not believe what we had just witnessed.

It turns out, about 2 hours earlier, when Mrs. Pravda was in the bathroom; she was faced with a dilemma. As she walked into the bathroom after she hit her tee shot, she put her brand new monogrammed golf glove in her back pocket. This is not unusual, as most put it there in between shots, or on their golf bag. As she lowered her shorts to use the facilities, unbeknownst to her, the birthday present slipped loose and fell into the toilet. As she got rid of the lobster and fillet and the rest of her dinner celebration, it landed right on top of the glove. She did not notice this until she was finished. Now she said she had a dilemma. If she flushed the toilet the glove could cause the toilet to get clogged up and over flow. When they would call maintenance to fix the clog they will find a glove. Unfortunately, since it has her initials on it they would trace it back to her and it will be an event that will haunt her forever. So she knew she had to think of something else. She decided to take a paper towel and reach into the toilet and remove the glove. Once she did, she flushed the toilet and the birthday celebration dinner made its way to the dump.

Now she knew she was taking too long and didn't

want her group to wait for her forever. So she started to panic a little bit. She wrapped the glove up in the paper towel and rushed out of the bathroom. She failed to see the large trash can that was to her left as she exited the facilities. As she bounced down the fairway she saw me and asked if I could throw it away. The rest you already know...........

AIR WOLF

I wanted to write this story not to brag about what I did, but to let you know about the generosity of one of our members. By the end of this story, you will see, (as do many), this gentleman has a heart as large as Secretariat.

Let me begin by telling you that I was on my way to the Hamptons for the Spring and Summer of 2011. On my way from Florida, I stopped in Baltimore to see my family. And in case you were wondering, yes my mom always makes Maryland Crab Cakes for me when I visit. If you have not had them, I suggest you try them the next time you are in Baltimore. Although mom would gladly make them for you, I suggest you try them at a local restaurant. You will not be disappointed.

While I was at my parent's house, I received a

phone call from my friend Jon. He was wondering what time I was going to arrive in town because one of the owners of the golf club I was working at was looking for company to go to the New York Knicks game on Wednesday evening. I told him I was leaving early that morning and could be in town by 1:00 pm. He said that would work, and he would pick me up at my house at about 3:30 and we would meet Benny and Barry and the four of us would head to the game. I was extremely excited because I had never been to Madison Square Garden before.

The entire drive from Baltimore to East Hampton was a bit nerve racking for me for the simple fact that I know it takes about 2-3 hours to get to the city from the Hamptons. If I was late that would certainly present a problem. Also I was so excited about the game; the drive seemed to take forever. Upon arriving at the club I said a few hello's to my friends that were already there and proceeded to my house to unpack my things. When Jon arrived at my house to pick me up, he mentioned that we would not be driving to the game this evening. Well I was somewhat disappointed, but I know things come up and plans change. So I asked him what we should do since we were not going to the game. He then corrected me, as he often does, and said, "I said we are not driving to the game. We are still going. We are taking Benny's helicopter!" I could not believe my ears! We are flying from East Hampton to Madison Square Garden in a helicopter. This was unbelievable! I jumped higher than Michael Jordan making a dunk. It was probably more like Phil Michelson's leap when he won the Masters, but it felt like MJ.

Now this was no ordinary helicopter. This was an Agusta 119 helicopter. One of the fastest non-military helicopters made in the world. The drive to the airport only took 10 minutes and from that point on, time seemed to fly for me. I can tell you now, before this story is over, that this day was going to be one of the Top 10 days in my life. As we arrived at the airport, Benny and Barry jumped out of their Escalade and Jon and I hopped out of his car and walked to the helicopter. Benny said hello, and asked if I would like to sit up front with the pilot. I said of course, I mean how often do you get the chance to fly in a helicopter, let alone sit up front. I later found out how much of a privilege this was, as Benny likes to sit in the front. I can now see why. The pilot Al handed me a headset, and walked me through everything he was doing. After he did his pre-flight check and his run-up, he began talking to the tower to get clearance for our journey. As the rotors kicked in we gently lifted off and hovered down the runway at 20 feet. As the powerful Agusta 119 made its way down the runway we slowly climbed with the grace and power of a Red Tail Hawk. In a matter of minutes we were cruising at approximately 155 mph at an altitude of 2500 feet. Al began to talk to us through the headsets and Benny told him to fix the squelch. It was bothering the guys in the back. Al got right on it and I proceeded to ask him about the Agusta and he commented how much he liked flying this helicopter and working for Benny.

The views were awesome. I was at 2500 feet looking down at the road I was just on a few hours ago. At about the halfway point, which was 25 minutes, (I know, hard to believe the entire flight was only going to be 50 minutes) Al asked me if I would like to take over the controls and fly the helicopter for a few minutes. This was an opportunity I did not want to pass up. After an excellent tutorial, Al let me take the controls for a few miles. Don't worry, Al is a professional and he would not let me get too far off course. He gave me a target to shoot for on the horizon which was three smoke stacks just past North Port.

I tried to keep her straight and level by using a combination of the stick, the rotors and the power. As I looked down, I noticed 737's taking off below us. What a sight. As we neared our destination Al mentioned that "he had the controls" and he would take us in from here. The feeling of flying that helicopter, if only for a brief few minutes, while under the guidance of a veteran pilot, was absolutely awesome.

Al slowly brought us down, and let me tell you, the view of the City of New York was absolutely sensational. The sun bouncing off of the buildings and the skyline was, what I thought, the best possible view of the city, ever. I would soon find out that I was wrong.

As we came over the Hudson River, Al landed the Agusta on the 10 x 10 helipad like a butterfly with sore feet. As we exited, we only had to take 15 steps, and we were swept into a waiting Escalade with what turned out to be the best driver in New York City, Bob. As we drove through the city it seemed like absolute pandemonium. People were everywhere. Stop lights did not matter, police officers telling drivers and pedestrians which way to go was of no concern. People in NYC had an agenda and no one was going to stop them. With all of this going on, Bob navigated with surgical precision.

I realized that we still had 2 hours before the game started and was curious as to where we were going. Benny said that we were going to have dinner at the Strip House before the game. I had been to this particular restaurant last year and remembered having a spectacular time. I was invited last year by Greg and Jill and enjoyed the dinner, the company and the atmosphere.

As we sat down, I was looking forward to hearing some of Barry's stories. I have never laughed so hard in my life as I did when Barry told me the raccoon story. I am not going to tell it here because there is no way I could do it justice. You have to make a point to sit down with Barry and let him tell it, your stomach will ache for days. The dinner at the Strip house was delicious and the stories did not disappoint. These are the days that you cherish in life. When you are surrounded with your family or friends and you look across the table and they are smiling back at you, life does not get any better.

As we walked out of the Strip House, Bob was waiting with the Escalade out front about 7 feet away. Into the vehicle and off to Madison Square Garden we went. He drove thru the streets like an

Olympic gold medalist skiing down a mountain. Most drivers would drop you off where it is convenient for them. With Bob, I would not be surprised if he drove the Escalade into MSG and dropped us off at our seats!

Well, he didn't drive us into the garden, but he got us closer than any other driver could. We said our goodbyes and he told Benny exactly where he would be when the game was over.

Our seats were nothing short of excellent. Just off of the floor, in line with the top of the key. We all sat down and watched the warm ups. You get a better appreciation of how good these guys really are when you see them up close. The entire garden was electric. Men were on their blackberry's, probably confirming the business deals from the day. Women were walking around dressed as if they were getting ready for the red carpet. There was so much activity to watch, Jon and I couldn't see straight.

As the game started the crowd began to voice their opinion of the game. And let me tell you, New York fans are not only well versed in there sports knowledge, they are not afraid to tell you how they feel at any given moment. This was supposed to be an "easy" home win against the New Jersey Nets. However, the Knicks forgot how to play defense this particular first half. And boy when they came back down the court after giving up an easy lay up, or wide open three pointer, the crowd let them have it. The entire first half was a shooting fest with no defense from either team. The first half came to an end with the Knicks trailing by 10. The halftime activities were great. Benny and Barry were discussing some changes to their golf course while Jon and I watched all the women at the game. The rest of the fans left for the concession stands. One of the halftime events featured two kids that were about six years old. They had to dribble the basketball from one end of the court to the other and back. Along the way, they had to dress in a players NBA uniform. Needless to say, by the time they put the size 13 shoes on; it became comical watching them dribble the ball down the court. As halftime came to an end and the game resumed, the crowd let the team know what was going to happen to them if they lost the game. Well, for a while, the team seemed to respond and they cut the lead to 6 as the fourth quarter started. I took me a moment to look around and reflect on just how lucky I was. Here I was on basically my first day before work, flying to NYC, sitting court side at MSG, with my friend Jon, and the owners of our golf course. Simply put, WOW!

The fans made a concerted effort to will the team to a victory. And with 14 seconds to go the Knicks took the lead which they would not relinquish. My first game at MSG was a winner, in more ways than one. Out the door and across the street was Bob. We hopped in the Escalade and Bob whisked us back to the chopper. I believe Bob drove us 3 miles in less then 45 seconds. I know, I know, but it seemed fast. Barry sat up front and Jon, Benny and I slid into the back. As Al flew the helicopter across the river, I looked out to see the city in the night. It was mesmerizing. The buildings seemed to leap into the sky and the lights pierced the clouds. The city that never sleeps was creating dreams for many others than just me that evening. The flight back was very peaceful. We had a tail wind so we reached the airport in just less than 40 minutes. Al again landed the helicopter as softly as before. As we left I said goodbye to Barry and Benny.

Thanking Benny a million times would not have been enough. But somehow I think he knows how much that day meant to me. I told Jon on the way home that this was a day I would cherish forever because of the people I spent it with.

MAGICAL ROUND

Sometimes the outcome is not the story; it is the journey to accomplish the goal. I would like to take you thru a magical round as a player broke the 400 barrier for an 18 hole round of golf. In this chapter you will be called upon to visualize shots that will make your brain ache. Your nose will scrunch up and you will be telling yourself, NO WAY! Trust me my friends, I would not believe any of this myself, unless I was on the bag. So sit back and enjoy this one.

My player today is Mr. Finkle, who is not a member but a guest for the day playing on a gift certificate. Typically the club donates these gift certificates to charitable organizations and they are bid on at silent auctions with the proceeds going to a local charity. Mr. Finkle is the beneficiary of one of those certificates and my job today was to make sure he enjoyed himself.

We ventured to the range to warm up on a beautiful September day. As you looked around you were hard pressed to try and find a cloud. The temperature was a perfect 77 degrees and we had just a breath of wind blowing in from the west. The range was set up perfectly. Titleist golf balls were stacked in piles that looked like the ancient pyramids. There were 10 stations set up for the members to hit from, however 9 would remain empty and untouched, as we were the only ones on the course.......for now. Mr. Finkle bent down to do a few stretches, and then proceeded to reach for his driver. I handed him a tee and he put a golf ball on it and prepared to launch it down the range. As he took his first practice swing, he was just a little too close to the ball and accidentally hit it. It went flying sideways and destroyed the pyramid next to us. Balls went screaming everywhere. For such a quiet morning, we just turned the volume up a bit. We had not even hit a ball down the range yet and the driving range looked like the juniors had been there for a week already. After some drives, irons, chip shots, and some putts, we were ready to tempt fate. Yes, we were going to play an entire 18 hole round of golf. I walked to the first tee armed with a bag of 14 clubs, some tees, a scorecard, and enough golf balls to start my own distribution center.

Our first hole was a par 4 which measured 454 yards in length. It's a dog leg to the right and it's about 225 yards to carry the corner. Mr. Finkle teed his golf ball up and after a practice swing, proceeded to rifle his first, second, third and fourth shots directly into the woods. His fifth ball went down the right center of the fairway and stopped just short of the bunker where we lay 9. We walked up to the shot and together we determined we should just hit an 8 iron over the bunker and put the ball in the middle of the dog leg. Well Mr. Finkle bladed the ball and it buried itself in the lip like an Alabama tick on a coon dog. After some heavy excavation, an unplayable, and a few swings in the bunker, we were laying 17 in the middle of the fairway at the 169 yard marker. The next swing was a whiff. A whiff is when a player just completely misses a golf ball. For scoring purposes in this round, I was told to count every swing, penalty and lost ball. A five wood and a lob wedge later, we were on the green. A smooth 3 putt and we finished number one with a 23.

We only needed to take a few steps to reach hole number two. A 281 yard par 4 in which the fairway slopes from right to left. Most players will take out a driver and try to put the ball on the green. We had the same thought process, but our first two balls when across the street and out of bounds. Our third golf ball had a chance to reach the green for a minute, then gravity took over and we had 151 yards left. I know, you do the math.

Our next attempt was a top. A top is when a player takes a swing but the club only hit's the top portion of the golf ball. Nothing good ever comes from a shot like this. We did a few deep breathing exercises and we put two shots together. However they were a whiff and a top which landed us in the bunker of death. Needless to say, we don't like bunkers. After what seemed to be enough time to build a few sand castles, we were on the green again laying 15. Our putting was pretty consistent and we walked off of the hole with an easy 18.

We improved on this hole by 5 strokes. Things were looking up until we reached the 414 yard par 4. This particular hole challenges the player with two bunkers in the middle of the fairway and out of bounds on the right. You can hit the ball anywhere you like, on this hole, just not in the bunkers. If you haven't realized it by now, this is the kind of player you can never ever take your eyes off of. The ball could go anywhere at any time. And this tee shot was one of those times. I was standing directly across from my player. Some would say our belly buttons were facing each other. As Mr. Finkle gave the golf ball a descending blow, the club slipped in this hands and the face was wide open. This sent the golf ball rattling around the golf bag like a bb in a tin can. I fell backwards; the clubs hit the ground and Mr. Finkle screamed like he saw a ghost. Luckily, everyone was fine except for the golf ball. But that did not matter as its life was coming to an end as it was launched out of bounds on the next shot.

I would describe the next few series of shots as Whiff- Whiff-Top-Top- Zing! You figured it out. We missed twice, topped two more and sent the fifth shot heading towards the out of bounds fence. Lucky for us, it hit the middle rail of the white fence and rolled right back into the fairway.

When you're chasing history, you need a little bit of luck. Three putts later we carded a 21.

A 170 yard par three lay waiting for us next. We took out our driver like we just finished Q-School. This particular shot went 203 yards straight left. Although we avoided the bunkers on the third hole as recommended, our ball managed to find its way in there. Problem was, we were on hole 4 and our ball was not. I gave Mr. Finkle another ball and we played that one as a lost ball. This scenario would repeat itself more than once on this historic round. The next tee shot went a foot. We teed it up again and sent a laser beam into the greenside bunker. Two damn-its, and three son of a bitches later and we were laying 17 three feet from the hole. We lagged up number 18 to six inches and tapped in number 19.

Number 5 is a spectacular 559 yard par 5. It has a giant waste bunker down the right side and fescue you could lose a car in on the left. Next to the waste bunker on the right is a beautiful comfort station. The bathrooms are immaculate and you can get a frosty beverage or a snack if you like. Most players will hit their tee shots down the middle of the fairway and walk over and grab something. We were going to visit the comfort station, but not in the same manner most members do. Two whiffs on the tee box lead to a Zoweee heading right towards the comfort station. Luckily for the fortified brick walls, 25 yards of fescue stopped our golf ball from a head on collision...... for the moment. We found the ball and tried to pitch it out to the fairway to no avail. The fescue grabbed the club and the ball bounced off of the wall and landed right in the middle of the forward tee box. Sometimes they say you have to take a few steps backwards in order to go forwards. In our case it was 47 yards. We walked back to hit the ball into the fairway and Mr. Finkle took a stroll over to the bathroom.

We had a little motivational meeting before the next shot and it worked. Mr. Finkle hit the ball dead solid perfect. It flew down the fairway and nestled itself next to the 214 yard marker. I knew it was a challenge for us to put a few good shots together back to back. But one can only hope. Well as it turned out, I ran out of luck and got a Whiff-Top-Whiff- Top-Zinggggg!

I had an idea of where the ball went but it was going to be tough to find. I looked for it as long as it took to rescue the Chilean Miners but this ball was not to be found. We dropped another one where we thought it might have been and we hit the ball up close to the fringe of the green, along with enough fescue to hide a dinosaur. We chipped the ball up to about 10 feet and a Ping-Pong match began. Mr. Finkle putted the ball from one side to the other and the ball never even sniffed the hole. I felt like I was watching the USA vs. Taiwan in the 1999 Table Tennis World

Championships. The ball finally went in and left us with a 26. Just a side note, this is the number 1 handicapped hole on the golf course. Like that made any difference at all.

Upon reaching the sixth hole which is a par 3 of approximately 157 yards, I picked up some broken tees and filled up some divots. The divot mix is kept in a brown wooden box that is about 2 feet by 2 feet in length. We have them on all the par 3 tee boxes. I walked off the yardage, figured in the wind, gauged the uphill and had all of that information ready as Mr. Finkle approached the teeing ground. With all the calculations and computations, we decided on a 5 wood. Wrong club!

This ball was heading left immediately but only 7 feet off of the ground. It found the side of a hill about 70 yards away in less than a second. Now this hill should not be in play............for anyone. So when we arrived we found his ball half way up the hill. With his age, athletic ability and the position of the ball, pure physics would not allow him to hit the ball, ever. But this did not stop him for a second. He asked for his lob wedge and the games began. Now with this stance he could hit a 2 iron and the slope of this hill would have turned it into a sand wedge. But this topic was not up for discussion. He gave it the old college try, but the hill turned his golf swing into a baseball swing and the club just got lodged into the side of the slope, 12 consecutive times. We took an unplayable, chipped it up to the green, and after a few putts, we walked off with a 17. Not bad considering we only actually hit the ball twice.

The "perfect club", yes that was the actual name of the model, was designed to get you out of trouble if you were in the rough. Unfortunately, it did not work for us on number seven and what was worse, we took a safari on hole number eight. A 20 and a 27 were the scores for those two holes.

We were running out of energy as we approached the ninth hole. A devious 418 yard par four which calls for a well-placed tee shot and a pin point iron shot. We had neither. Our goal was to get to the beverage cart that was located behind the green. By doing so, we could grab an energy bar and a drink and head out to the back nine. Our first three tee shots dove into the fescue like a Japanese Kamikaze pilot in World War II. Our fourth shot put us in a position that we could actually do damage to the club house. Then again, we could do that from just about anywhere with our golf skills. The club house managed to escape the next shot, but a Mercedes in the parking lot was not so lucky. Our Titleist hit the roof with a loud thud, and then rolled around in the empty parking lot for a while. It seemed lonely there all by itself. However, it did not have to wait long until it had company. If there was one saving grace for the next shot, it did miss the Mercedes. We made mincemeat of the last 100 yards and when the smoke cleared and we were at the beverage cart, we had a 28 for number nine.

On hole number 10 we hit a deer and posted a 28.

Remember about 141 strokes ago I mentioned that this is the type of player that you can never take your eyes off of? Well I made that mistake on this hole. This 159 yard par three would prove to be a directional challenge for us this day. The first two shots went out of bounds and I lost the next 3. Our 11th shot finally came to rest on a dirt cart path. At this particular course you have to play the ball as it lies on the cart path. The lie was ok, so I handed Mr. Finkle his wedge and moved out of the way. As I turned my back for just a split second, Mr. Finkle swiveled his head around to zero in on the flag stick and take dead aim. His body adjusted to his new alignment and he started his back swing. Before I could say a word the ball was in the air. The problem was it was headed towards the maintenance building. You see, as he looked around for the flag stick his eyes locked in on the antenna on top of the maintenance building. This was the wrong time to hit a great shot. It ricocheted off of the vent at the top of the building and trickled down the parking lot and came to rest 10 feet from the original location. As Mr. Finkle began to address the ball again, I was able to yell to him and let him know that the green was "Over here!" Eight minutes later, we finished with a 24.

Although the 12th hole is short in length, it puts a premium on accuracy. It's one of the few holes out here that set up well for a left handed player that fades the ball. The two keys to playing this hole well are, put the ball in the fairway off the tee, and do not go into the waste bunker. We never touched the fairway. Our third tee shot whistled around in the trees for quite a while. Our next stop was the waste bunker you should never be in. After, 6 swings, our only way to get out of the waste bunker was to invoke Rule 27-4-AR from the USGA rule book, which states, "I have had enough, and we cannot get out of this bunker, so drop it on the green." That rule helped us finish with a 30.

A 418 yard dog leg right lay waiting for us next. There was no one on the course up until now, so on the previous 12 holes there was no need to yell "fore!" This quickly changed on this hole as groups were now making the turn and playing down number 10. I yelled "fore" five times. The group coming up number 10 was kind enough to tell me that "Hey, we heard you the first time." I said "I know, but we hit 5 balls over here." They could only respond by saying "Wow." We almost chipped it in for a 20, but finished with a 23.

The par 3 fourteenth is a difficult 180 yard hole. The part that made it difficult for us today was that you had to hit it at least 61 yards to clear the fescue and sticker bushes. A task that I thought we were up to today. Wrong again. As our tee shot found its way into the sticker bush lined fescue, Mr. Finkle ventured out to find it, and he did. Guess what club he asked for? You got it, the perfect club. I thought it would only take one swing to convince him that this was the wrong club, it took 5. On the even number swings the club got stuck on the vines and he fell into the sticker bushes. If he would have taken one more swing, he would have died by 1000 cuts. I called on Rule 27-4-AR again before he bled out. A 19 was entered on our card.

A beautiful par 4 awaited us next. We hit a drive that any PGA player would be proud of. It left the club like a rocket and climbed like the space shuttle. We both watched in utter amazement. It seemed to climb forever. When it came down it actually had some top spin on it and continued to roll down the middle of the fairway for another 9 yards. We started to high five each other like we just won the Masters. Our walk to the golf ball was awesome. We talked as if the first 14 holes did not exist. We discussed how we would play the remaining three holes and hoped for a par or a birdie. Reality came back with a vengeance and a WHIFF - WHIFF - TOP - TOP - ZING, followed by an out of bounds. An 18 was the best we could do.

A new tee box on number 16 provided us with a 29 as we side- stepped Armageddon on the evil 17th with a 10.

If you are keeping track of the score, you know that we have a chance to break 400 with only one hole to go. We will have to stay focused because 18 is an evil 281 yard dog leg left par 4. You have to hit it about 185 yards to clear the corner and have a wide open shot at the green. And we did..........in 11 shots. This is the smallest green on our golf course. It measures about 19 yards wide by about 17 yards deep. The front of the green has a false front, so anything on the edge of the green will roll 30 yards back into the fairway for another try. If you are left, right, or long, you are dead. The entire green is protected by bunkers that are extremely deep. Even if you do get out of the bunker, your golf ball will probably run off the green. We were hitting our 12th shot from the 84 yard marker, our 13th from the 67 yard marker, and our 14th from the 39 yard marker. We were gaining on the hole. Number 15 landed on the green and stayed. However it was on the back shelf and our hole was on the lower shelf. Barring a miracle, this next putt was going to go off the green and stop right next to the marker we just hit from. He just had to touch it to get the ball over the hill, and he did. But gravity took over and the putt gained speed going down the hill. We both started to beg and plead for the ball to slow down or stop. It slowed down to a crawl, but not enough. As it got ready to roll off of the green and through the fringe and down the fairway, a miracle did happen! It rolled into a sprinkler head and stopped. A free drop and a three putt and we finished the hole with a 19. I removed my hat and thanked Mr. Finkle and we walked towards the club house. At the club house, he added up his score and it came to 399. He couldn't believe his eyes. You would have thought he was looking at his first born child he was so proud. His eyes started to well up a little and we said our goodbyes. As I walked home for the day my only thought was, "History in the making, and I was part of it. What a privilege!"

CADDIE TRAINING SIR!

In my career, I have also had the opportunity to train new caddies, thousands of them. When a course decides that they want to add a caddie experience for a client as an option, I travel to the property to train them. Once they come to training, they have already been through a written test, a personality test and a group interview. If they make it through all of that, they are invited to training class. Training usually consists of five days. Each day is approximately four hours long and lasts about 9 holes. They carry a player's bag and we discuss various topics depending on where the player is located. For example, on the tee box, we make sure to place the bag one yard outside and one yard behind the right tee marker that the players are teeing off from. When they are walking down the fairway, we tell them to locate the golf ball, calculate the yardage for the player, and place the bag down before the player arrives. When they get to the green we tell them to fix a players pitch mark, clean their golf ball, have a read ready for them in case they ask, attend the flag stick, and anything else they may need on the green.

Our story begins with a new trainee, Brad. As all of the new recruits for the day enter the classroom, they introduce themselves and we began to watch a video. The video is approximately an hour and a half long and it goes over everything a new recruit needs to know. The class starts promptly at 7:00 am; however we had to wait for Brad as he was late and finally arrived at 7:15. Strangely enough, he did not want to take off his sunglasses, which raised a yellow flag for me and the other trainers. It turns out that the reason he needed to leave his sunglasses on was because he was just coming in from a long night of partying and his eyes looked like small red laser beams.

After everyone sees the video, we then take them out onto the golf course to demonstrate everything that they just saw in the film. We do this because some people learn from watching a video, and some people learn from direct demonstrations. We give them both options in hopes that it will be beneficial down the road. After we are done with the live demonstrations we go out in a group of 4 players. Each trainee will carry a trainer's golf bag for a few holes. If we have more than 4 trainees in a group, some will observe while the others carry the bag. After a few holes, we will switch trainees so everyone in the group gets a chance to caddie. On this particular morning, we only had 4 potential caddies in the class so each one would carry a bag for nine holes.

I had Brad carry my bag for nine holes, and of course, here is where the story begins. The first hole was a 379 yard par four. Most players would not hit a driver on this hole because it might go thru the fairway. I don't hit my driver as far as most players so I teed up the ball and hit it down the left center about 225 yards. As Brad went out to find my yardage, he located the marker and began his process. However, in this case the marker that Brad was using was in front of my ball. He walked from the marker to my ball and then gave me my yardage. Brad missed the marker earlier in the fairway before my golf ball which caused him to make two mistakes.

The marker that Brad was referencing was the 150 yard plate. He proceeded to walk 11 paces back to my ball and tell me that I had 139 yards to the middle of the green. I reminded Brad, in a nice way that we should walk from the marker to the ball, while we are facing the green. This way, we already have the yardage by the time we arrive at the player's ball. He missed the marker that was behind the ball. Many new caddies do this also and it is not a huge deal on the first day. However, when they use the marker in front of the ball, they always turn around to walk back to the ball and in every single instance they subtract the yardage they walked off, instead of adding it. In this instance Brad subtracted 11 from 150 instead of adding 11 to 150. So his incorrect yardage of 139 was actually 161. We took a little time out to address this issue in hopes that this would be the only time it happened to the group.

The next hole was a short par 4. It measured 335 yards and turned ever so slightly right to left. All of the trainers hit and the caddies headed down the fairway to find their player's golf ball and calculate their yardages. Brad seemed to be more concerned with talking to the other caddies than he was in finding my ball and getting my yardage. I arrived at my ball before my caddie did, this should never happen when you are caddying for only 1 player. I told Brad that this was still a job interview and he would do better to pay attention. Brad shrugged it off and I began to think he was not someone we were looking to hire. We all hit our shots at the flag; the caddies fixed our divots and made their way to the green. All of the caddies put their player's bags off to the side and began working the green. First they would fix pitch marks, and then clean a player's golf ball while reading their putt. If the player was far enough away from the hole, the caddie would attend the flag stick. My putt broke about 3 feet left to right. When I asked Brad what he thought, he said "straight in." Now I knew that not only was he bad at calculating yardages, he could not read a green to save his life. The chance of his training lasting beyond today was ZERO, at best. We finished the hole, one of the caddies put the flag stick back in, and we headed to the next hole.

The next tee box was extremely elevated so we

had to walk up the side of the hill. As we arrived, the caddies lined up the golf bags perfectly. The problem was there were 4 players, 4 caddies, but only 3 bags. Brad had just lost my golf bag. He nervously tried to take the bag that was next to him, but Jess, the caddie for Andy the other trainer, quickly told him to get lost, this was her bag. He started to look dazed and confused when I asked him for my driver. "Brad, where is my golf bag," I asked. He looked down below at the previous green, but he couldn't see it. It was there. He left it next to a tree and in all of the commotion when leaving the green; he just got lost in conversation and walked to the tee box without the golf bag.

Now as he looked down, it was obscured by a large oak tree. Brad said, "I don't remember where I put it." I told him to use his head and go back down to the previous green and look around. Chances are, it's down there somewhere. Well he left on his quest to find the bag and we all had a good laugh at his expense. Anyway, this was going to be his first and last day.

We were extremely shocked when Brad showed up for the second day of training. All of the trainers discussed cutting him from the class, the problem was, there was a miscommunication as to who was going to do it, and it never got done. Whoops. If there was one bright spot for today, Brad was only 10 minutes late this day. On this training day we were going to give each of the caddie's two bags. In this instance, 2 trainees would caddie for a few holes and 2 trainees would observe. After a few holes they would switch. There was no way in the world Brad was going to go first. He was horrible and it would take forever for him to do a few holes. Since he was here, we would give him a shot at double bag. Big mistake! Brad could not keep track of one player, he was slow, had a hard time doing simple addition and subtraction, and had a difficult time multi-tasking. How in the hell this guy got through the interview process is a miracle. Then again, some managers don't have the heart to tell people they are not cut out for the job. I guess that is why over the years I have had recruits with one arm missing, over 400 pounds, no golf knowledge whatsoever, and a blind individual. I get tasked with the responsibility of making them go through training then telling them they are not qualified. But I leave that for another book.

Brad got an opportunity to carry two bags for one entire hole and the circus began. He put the bags on the wrong tee box, he went to the wrong players golf ball, he put the left handed players clubs in the right handed players bag (very hard to do) and made about a million other mistakes. The end of his caddie training career came when one of his players was in a bunker. He placed both bags down, and he put them on the side of a slope instead of at the bottom of the bunker. As he leaned into the bunker to grab a rake, the bags of golf clubs stood behind him, for only a few more seconds. He stood up with the rake then lost his balance. He tried to use the rake to regain his balance much like a tight rope walker does. However, as he swung the rake around, the teeth got stuck in the far bag's strap and the roller coaster began. The far bag hit the near bag and the rake pulled them both into the bunker. Brad hit the bottom of the bunker first.

The clubs and the bags seem to defy gravity for just a moment. The entire scene looked like the room in Poltergeist when everything is flying around. The clubs were traveling in every possible direction. When the empty bags landed on Brad I would had said that the only thing hurt was his pride, but he didn't have any. The next few moments were hilarious as the clubs seemed to bury him little by little.

After digging Brad out from the bunker and putting the clubs back in the proper bags, I called the manager of the property and asked him to bring out a golf cart so we could ride Brad back into the clubhouse and discuss the end of his short lived caddie career. Brian brought out one of the older models with no front windshield and a broken rear bumper. As Brian arrived I told him about the events for the past two days and we both agreed to take him in and cut him from training.

Now, when you have three people in a golf cart, the extra person can ride on the back, or sit on the front dash board facing the passenger and hold on to the steering column and the roof support. In this instance, the back bumper was broken so Brad sat on the dash board facing me.

As we headed back to the clubhouse Brian took a right a little too fast. As the right front wheel went into a hole, the entire golf cart lunged forward and Brad shot through the spot where a windshield should be and landed on the pavement in front of the golf cart. Brian tried to hit the brakes but the cart did not respond in time and we ran over Brad. He was not hurt at all but we did have to dust off the tire mark that covered his body. The next 13 minutes were spent trying to get Brad to stop crying. He was babbling like a 6 month old that hasn't had their diaper changed for a week. Honest to goodness, it was embarrassing. As we sat Brad down in the office we realized that we could not cut the guy from training after we just ran over him. There had to be some kind of rule about that. So we told him he could come back tomorrow and try again. However, if he made just one mistake, his career would really be over this time. Brad went home and we went to dinner and laughed until we cried.

The following morning was forecaddie training. This is where the caddie runs ahead of his players approximately 150 yards. They get the yardages before the players arrive, then after they hit the caddie fills their divots and hustles to the green. On the green the caddies takes care of their regular duties as well as holding any extra clubs the players may have brought to the green. For some players that miss the green and end up in a bunker or in the rough, they may have their putters along with a sand wedge or a 7 iron. The caddie will hold these clubs along with the flag stick until the hole is done. Then the caddie will put the flag stick back in, give back the remaining clubs and describe the next hole.

Brad finished the hole and headed down the fairway to his forecaddie position. He was 150 yards down the fairway when his career came to a grinding halt. This time it was over for good.

Instead of us hitting our tee shots we waved for Brad to come back. As he slowly approached the tee box, he was both puzzled and out of breath. He said "I did everything perfect, there is no way I made a mistake on that hole. Why did you make me run all the way out there, then all the way back in? What could you possibly want this time?" I said "It's not me that wants anything. The group behind us might want that flag stick when they play that hole!" You see, Brad forgot to put the flag stick back in the hole and took it with him all the way out to the fairway. Bruised, battered, and run over, Brad left for a new career.

THE LARGEST TIP EVER

There are some days when you just watch and listen and take it all in. This was one of those days because the gentleman that I was about to caddie for, Mr. Cashman, just sold his business for 17 million dollars. He wanted to play alone so we hopped in a cart and headed down to the range. This is where you get an opportunity to see how your player hits the ball, and in general make conversation with them.

As he launched the balls down the range, he informed me that this was the greatest day in life as he had just sold his business for 17 million dollars and bought himself a new BMW. Immediately I knew two things were going to happen today. I would not get tipped a penny and this would be a great story. I was right on both. I have caddied for thousands and thousands of rounds and there are a few statements that scare the living hell out of a caddie when it comes to receiving a good tip. Now keep in mind, 99.9 percent of the players are awesome when it comes to tipping. Here we are only talking about the .1 percent. Some of those statements that scare a caddie are as follows:

"Where is the ATM machine?"

"What's the biggest tip you ever got?"

"You were the best caddie I ever had!"

"Can I charge your tip to my room?"

"Do you have change for a $5?"

"My partner already tipped for both of us, right?"

"I just made a killing in the market!"

"This is the best I have ever played!"

He finished warming up and we headed to the first tee. On the way we stopped for two Vodka and Sprites. I know what you are thinking, one for me and one for him. Well you would be incorrect. He finished the first one off before we reached the tee box. On the tee box he told me that he just purchased a 2010 BMW for about half a million dollars. He wanted to make sure that I knew that he paid cash for it. So he told me about three times before he smashed one down the middle of the fairway. This was a loop in which I just drove him around in a cart. We drove to his golf ball and he told me about some of the features in his new car. He said "This car is Awesome; you have to see it when we are done."

We finished the first hole and the second Vodka drink at the exact same time that the beverage cart came around. Jessica poured two more drinks as she was told of all the special features of the half a million dollar car. Mr. Cashman asked her to check on us every few holes because he was really going to party while playing this 18 hole round.

I don't know what went quicker, the second and third hole, or the third and fourth drink. Anyway I was informed that the car had a special security system that detected a person's heartbeat if they were in your car. Knowing this, you could inform the police and they could get the car thief before he gets you. My response was "How good is the security system, if someone can get in your locked car?" He had no response.

Jessica arrived just in time to refill Mr. Cashman's drink. He asked for 2 more and while he was sipping the first one I yelled "cannon ball!" When a caddie yells cannon ball, that means that the person is supposed to drink the entire beverage without stopping. He was a good sport and finished it in the blink of an eye.

The next hole we discussed how fast his car was. As the alcohol kicked in so did the exaggerations. He told me the car would go 235 mph on the highway and I told him that I was 6 foot tall, (I'm only 5'5" tall on a good day), we made it to the turn and I suggested that he might want to get a sandwich or a burger before we ventured to the back nine. Bad idea. I was informed that the food would counteract the alcohol. What a waste of a good buzz he said, as we loaded up our cart with 2 more Vodka and Sprites and drove to number 10. At this point in time he would not pass the breathalyzer test, so it was a good thing that I was driving. The next feature that we talked about was his "run flat" tires. He mentioned that the run flat tires would enable him to drive over 200 miles to get to the nearest service center to repair it. I asked him "if that is the case, why do you have a spare?" He had no response.

During the consumption of the next few Vodka and Sprites I found out some more great information about the car. You could open the car with your cell phone; if it started to rain it would automatically put the top up, it did not have any blind spots, and it had an automatic collision avoidance system. Since he was smashed I figured I would have a little fun. I replied, "Mine has the same features. I have keys, I check the weather report, I look into my mirrors before I turn, and if I am close to someone I step on these space age inventions called brakes." He had no response.

The round ended and Mr. Cashman dusted off a total of 14 Vodka and Sprites in a matter of two and a half hours. He could hardly stand up as he poured himself out of the cart. He started wobbling and could not catch his balance. He went side to side for what seemed to be an eternity before landing in the freshly planted and very colorful tulip bed. I was laughing hysterically…..on the inside. I helped him up and he insisted that he show the car to me. I said on one condition, no driving it. I would have the shuttle service drive him back around to the other side of the hotel and have someone take him up to the room. He agreed.

We walked over to his car and he regurgitated all of the special features of the car. Not one of them made any sense. We stood next to the car and he proceeded to tell me that I should check out the inside. He reached into his pocket and pulled out what I thought were his keys but it was his cell phone. Although he told me he could open the car with his phone, I know he was looking for his keys with the remote control.

He pushed the number 5 key on the phone and

nothing happened. Then he waited a few seconds and tried again. I didn't have the heart to tell him that his keys were still in the golf bag. Two more tries and the car started to get verbally abused.

He yelled, "You damn half a million dollar piece of crap. I own you for one day and you're broke already. I should take you back to the dealer and get my cash back!" He then threw the phone with all of his might at the driver side window and one of the cars security features kicked in. You see, the windows were cell phone resistant. The cell phone ricocheted off the window and hit him dead solid perfect in the middle of the forehead. Mr. Cashman hit the pavement like a sack of potatoes.

The hotel sent their security and first aid teams and carted Mr. Cashman back to a secret area where they make sure their guests are ok. I went home with no tip, but a phenomenal story, which was just fine with me.

CADDIE NICKNAMES

Just about all of the caddies working on tour, or at a private golf club have a nickname. Mine is "The Squirrel". I hope that all goes well with this book and I will explain how I received that nickname in Caddy Tales 2. In this story I would like to tell you how a caddie lost his original nickname and received a new one at the end of the day.

I was working on this beautiful Saturday with "The Rocket". He gave the nickname to himself because he said he was FAST. I worked with him on a few occasions and he was anything but fast. One would say he is so slow that it takes him an hour and a half to watch 60 Minutes. The Rocket also had a tendency to let his players know how good he is before they ever go out on the course. Now over the course of a decade, I have learned that you let your player bring you into their group. As soon as you start telling a player how good you are, or what your credentials are, that usually creates a little friction in the group. After all, go show them that you can do a great job, don't tell them. A caddie needs to realize that it is a privilege to be in the group, not an inalienable right.

After our introductions we each picked up two players golf bags and headed to number one tee. The entire time The Rocket complained about the weight of one of his bags. I told him I would gladly switch with him before we teed off of number one. He thought about it for a while then decided against it because his player with the heavy bag looked like a big tipper. How in the world he came up with that one I will never know. I don't have the super powers necessary to tell which players are big tippers in advance.

As we reached the first tee The Rocket gave the

group a brief description of the hole and he also told the players where they should hit their tee shots. Now that should have been the end of the conversation. The Rocket then proceeded to tell the players that he was a scratch golfer and on this hole he usually takes an aggressive line and hits it over the boulder on the right. Because he has a 300 yard drive, he can cut the corner. The four players looked at me and rolled their eyes. I just shrugged my shoulders.

We reached the second hole and The Rocket started to give his little speech about where regular players should hit the golf ball and players like himself should hit the golf ball, but Mr. McDaniel's cut him off pretty quick. I thought that was awesome. The beverage cart arrived while we were on this hole and The Rocket decided to go above and beyond with his customer service and make sure everyone was taken care of. He went over to the cart and started a small conversation. The problem was he took both of his player's bags over there and they had not even hit their approach shots. So the guests had to get their own yardage and come to the cart to get a club to hit. This was not a pleasant experience.

The next incident happened on a long par 5. We handed our players their drivers and took a short cut to the fairway. Our players were going to stop at the restroom so we had a little time before they arrived. The Rocket took a golf ball out of his player's bag and started chipping the ball back and forth in the rough. This is a definite no-no. The sad part about this loop aside from his two players having a terrible experience is that The Rocket does not feel he is doing anything wrong. He thinks he is giving great service.

As we made the turn, the weight of the bags were taking a toll on The Rocket. Now don't feel bad for him. These bags were not heavy at all. The problem was he was walking 600 yards on every hole when 400 would have been sufficient. You see he was making all the rookie mistakes. They included: going to the wrong ball, not watching the ball when it was in the air, and forgetting to walk off yardage from the makers. So in general, he was about as inefficient as one could be. He was horrible.

Well we arrived on the 18th hole and his player had a putt to win the match. Mr. McDaniel's thought better of it, but he finally asked The Rocket for a read on his putt. The Rocket told him that he needed to hit this putt a foot to the left. Mr. McDaniel's said "Are you sure? You hardly bent down to take a look at it" The Rocket replied, "Sir, I am the best green reader this company has and I have seen this putt a hundred times. Just hit it a foot to the left." Well Mr. McDaniel's hit it exactly where The Rocket said and it moved a foot to the left. So when it stopped, it was two feet away from the hole. Without missing a beat The Rocket said, "I thought you understood what I meant. I meant it's going to go left." Whoops. Everyone in the group knew he was wrong and what made it worse was he tried to blame it on his player. Big mistake!

Now you may be thinking, why didn't I do anything. Two reasons. The first one is that caddies, or people like that, cannot take constructive criticism. They freak out and think that you are talking down to them. Second, by caddying next to him I looked like the best caddie in the world. My two players were saying thank goodness we got the other guy. And it never fails; the players pay you a little more when they feel they received a better caddie than their friends. This is where things get interesting.

Our players finished the round and started to put

their things away. They reached into the golf bags for their wallets and this was the moment of truth. Now when a caddie receives a tip, there are only two reasons he tells everyone else in the caddie house how much he made. They are either bragging or they are lying. The latter is most often the case. For this story, I need to share how much we each made. The recommended gratuity is $25.00 dollars and up depending on the level of service. So basically the minimum is 25 bucks and the sky is the limit if a player had a phenomenal day. The Rocket received a total of $50.00 dollars and I received a total of $ 200.00. We did not know what we received until we were back in the caddy shack because you never count you money in front of your players. The Rocket counted his and he had a high speed come apart.

The Rocket was infuriated. He had no idea why he received the minimum. I tried to tell him that one of the reasons he received the minimum was because he sucked. But he would have none of that. The more he thought about it the angrier he was. So he decided that he would go talk to his players and tell them how much he is supposed to make.

Huge mistake!

The Rocket met his players on the practice putting green as they were waiting for their other friends to finish before they took the shuttle bus back to the hotel. Now I don't know how the conversation went while he was talking to his players, but I do know I did not see any of his players reach into their pockets for more cash. As well they shouldn't. The Rocket came storming back to the caddy shack. He was so mad that no one could understand a word he was saying. It was awesome. He threw his towel across the room and kicked over a trash can. Then he grabbed his keys and left the building. He hopped in his car and went screeching down the road. Dirt and smoke was flying everywhere. By the way he was driving he looked like he could win the Daytona 500. The Rocket was gone.

The players jumped into the shuttle bus and headed back to the hotel. We grabbed our personal effects and started to leave when a message came over the radio asking for volunteers to help the maintenance department.

The Squirrel and "The Road Dog" (that name needs an entire chapter) took a cart to help maintenance. When we arrived it looked like they needed help with a stuck vehicle. The vehicle was The Rockets. He was driving too fast as he left the facility and skidded over the curb and into a ditch. He was not hurt, but his car was stuck in the mud. Only one wheel would turn and it was not gaining any traction. It looked like the car in My Cousin Vinny.

But wait, it gets better! As The Rocket is trying to get his car out of the ditch, who drives by? You guessed it, the shuttle bus with his players on it. They were leaning out the window yelling to The Rocket. "Thanks Rocket, hope everything is ok." I could not stop laughing. It was without a doubt one of the funniest moments I can remember. I did not finish helping as I was doubled over in pain from laughing too much.

As it turns out, the repairs cost him $509.00 dollars and the accident changed his nickname to CRASH!

MEMBER / GUEST

I have had the privilege of caddying at some of the most prestigious golf courses in the world. This story involves one of those facilities. This membership is so exclusive that even God himself is on the waiting list. Let me take you back to a Friday in late January. The temperature was a perfect 77 degrees and you could only see blue skies for miles around. I arrived at the course an hour early because I knew the check in procedure was going to be extremely strict. First I had to go thru a mandatory screening and finger printing. No red flags popped up on me so I was allowed to continue. Phew! Then it was off to the Facial Recognition System. I then signed my life away and proceeded to the Optical Scan Machine. My goodness, are we guarding the president or just caddying. The final security checkpoint was an office where I was to give a DNA sample. I was mistaken, because it was only a urine sample.

If the TSA wanted to learn something about how to screen an individual, they should take a lesson from this golf club. As I walked into the caddie shack I sat down and began to watch the show. Oh, and by the way, the caddie shack was state of the art. I could tell you some of the things that were in there, but I signed a confidentiality agreement and if I disclosed that information, they would remove my kidneys with a rusty fork.

Members at this particular course seemed to always arrive just one at a time as if it was Oscar Night in Hollywood. The first member rolled up in a in a 25 foot white stretch limousine. As this beast came up to the bag drop I watched intently because the geometry that would have to take place for this monster to turn around was quite complex. This member was soon topped by another who arrived in a 55 foot Hummer. No way does this "sleek black machine" make it to the bag drop. There were two other reasons this behemoth of a machine would not pull up to the bag drop area. In front of, and behind the Hummer were two Black Escalades. When the procession came to a stop, a total of 8 individuals got out of the Escalades and only one member got out of the Hummer. The eight were all dressed in dark suites, all had ear pieces in, and I know they were all carrying automatic weapons. For a minute I thought we were shooting a scene from Men in Black.

A Rolls Royce was next. Are you kidding me? Aren't those things about 600K? That's just my guess. But then again it's not like I'm shopping on E-Bay trying to find one. I probably can't even afford the radio controlled model. I never actually got a look at who jumped out of the Rolls, but I can bet you he was way more important than me. There was a break in the action for a few minutes when something raced across the sky. This was a little alarming at first because it was a plane and it was losing altitude quickly. Just what we needed, a plane crash just before our Member / Guest. But not to worry though, this was a Cessna 208 Caravan Sea Plane. One of the members was landing his Sea Plane in the adjacent lake. This was unbelievable. As you know from some of the previous stories, we caddies like to bet on anything. The bet was how the next member was going to arrive. By the way things were going, I was expecting the Space Shuttle to make an emergency landing right here on the 12th fairway. Well, none of us won, but we were quite impressed as a Sikorsky S-76D helicopter landed on the old driving range. Technology is a great thing as we all looked up the list price of the helicopter on our I-Phones. You can purchase a brand new one for the low price of $11.5 million dollars. If you pay cash instead of financing it, they will throw in a full tank of fuel for free. What a great deal. The show of financial global dominance ended as we watched a plane race across the sky. It was like a fly over before an NFL football game. Landing on the private airstrip next to the golf course was a Gulfstream GV. This baby will fly you and 14 of your closest friends from New York to Tokyo at an average speed of 600 mph. All you need to do is initiate a wire transfer from your bank for approximately $40 million dollars. I checked my bank account, and I am a little short.

As you can well imagine the prizes at this Member / Guest were going to be phenomenal. As we met our players we exchanged pleasantries and walked out to our respective holes. Today I had Mr. Peter Gale and Mr. John Bradley. I almost expected someone to parachute into the tournament, but that didn't happen. We played the first few holes and we learned of how a few of the members were forming a corporation to purchase the Planet Mars. I definitely want in on this Initial Public Offering when it becomes available. As we arrived at our first par 3 for the day we were met by two beautiful young ladies. They proceeded to talk to the members and they were even nice enough to offer them shots of Crop Cucumber Vodka. Both of my players indulged and commented on the deliciousness of the cocktail. On this particular par 3, which ever player was closest to the hole during the day would win a watch. Now this was no ordinary watch. Would you like to take a guess at the manufacture? You guessed it, a Rolex. And of course this was a Rolex – Daytona model number 116505. The case of this watch was 18K Rose Gold that measured 40mm in diameter. The bracelet was 18K Rose Gold Oyster with a flip-lock clasp. And the dial of this spectacular watch was black with luminous hour markers. The movement of the watch was classified as Oyster Perpetual Cosmograph. I think that means it is really expensive. Our trusty I-Phones told us that the list price of this piece of hardware was

$37,450.00. My two players hit their shots to the green but they were low bullets. They bounced off the green like we were skipping stones on a pond. No watch for us. There was a hole in one prize that was donated by one of the members. Any player that got a hole in one, on any hole would win 200 hours on Net Jets. A few searches on the I-Phone again and we found out that an hour on a jet is approximately $5,000.00 bucks. So a hole in one was worth a cool million dollars. Mr. Gale commented on the hole in one prize. "This is freaking great, I get a hole in one for the day and I will win the prize that I donated. It doesn't get any better than that."

A few holes later and we reached our second par three and we had a chance for another prize. This closest to the pin featured a prize that was literally out of this world. We actually had a chance at this one because it was only 167 yards. Enough about the hole already, let's get to the prize. At the end of the tournament, the player that was closest to the pin on this hole would receive a Zero Gravity Flying Experience for four people. Now let me tell you a little bit about this prize. The Zero Gravity Flying Experience is a once in a lifetime opportunity to experience true weightlessness. On a specially modified Boeing 727, parabolic arcs are performed to create a weightless environment allowing you to float, flip and soar as if you were in space. Specially trained pilots perform these aerobatic maneuvers which are not simulated in any way. As a passenger, you will experience true weightlessness. Checking the trusty I-Phone again, we found the price to be $5,197.50 per person. So which ever ball was closest to the hole for the day would garnish a floating day in space for $20,790.00. Mr. Gale commented on how he thought this might get him air sick, so he said if he won, I could have travel into space. I was extremely excited until one ball landed in the bunker and the other found the bottom of the pond. No space flight for me. "Nice job Pete," commented Mr. Bradley. "You get Scotty all excited about getting a space flight and you miss the green by about a decade! The least you could do is give him one of your cars."

About an hour went by before we reached our next par three. This hole was an absolute postcard. Standing on an elevated tee box the green looked like a private island. Mr. Gale and Mr. Bradley of course each had one of their own. Beautiful blue water guarded the front in case you came up short, while white sandy bunkers protected the perimeter. The hole measured 139 yards today and would probably play the number because there was just enough of a breeze to cancel out the downhill. Oh, by the way, did I mention what the prize was on this hole?

The closest to the pin on this hole was a television set. And as you could well imagine, it was not just a regular TV. Remember the days when you actually had to get up from your chair to change the channel? And there were only three major networks. Sure the TV had 13 numbers, but ten of them were just fuzzy. This was not one of those TV's. This was a Yalos Diamond from a small company that makes expensive stuff. As most of us know the TV is the centerpiece of most living rooms' and often the TV is the most expensive purchase for one's home theater system. If you really need to impress someone, you need either this TV, or Mr. Bradley's Black American Express Card. This extravagant television can be purchased in sizes up to 46". If Bob Barker wheeled this prize out on stage at "The Price is Right" and you bid $140,000.00, you would win an extra $100 bucks for guessing the exact price. We almost had a chance at the TV, but one of my player's golf balls decided to go scuba diving and the other went on vacation to the beach. Mr. Gale mentioned that this was seriously old technology as was a 3-D television. His house featured 16 hologram TV's. The last hologram I saw was when I was at Disney World and the ghost rode along in my cart during a ride in The Haunted Mansion.

After a couple of par fours and a par five, we came to our last hole of the day. It was a par three and we still had a shot at winning a closest to the pin prize. The winner on this hole would receive some clothes. I know, by now you're saying come on Scotty this is not going to be a regular golf shirt and a hat. You would be correct. A men's suit was the prize on this hole. And of course this was not just any suit. As we all know the modern suit first made its appearance in fashion during the late nineteenth century. While the fashion and style of suits have changed throughout the years, a suits power to signal rank and membership maintains. And in this suit you could not be more powerful. This was a Brioni

Vanquish II. In 2009 Brioni possibly the most renowned tailored manufacturer in the world released a stunner of a suit, the Brioni Vanquish II. These suits are of course made to measure and the fabric is woven from exotic fibers such as vicuña, pashmina, and Qiviuk. And don't worry if you are not familiar with those fibers. Those three fiber names eliminated 3 contestants at the 2012 National Spelling Bee. Oh, and by the way, the cost of the suit is a cool $43,000.00.

Mr. Bradley said, "Scotty, we have enough suits to clothe the entire country of Madagascar. If we win, you get the suit." Very generous. Mr. Gale took dead aim at this beautiful 188 yard par three. He connected with his hybrid but gave the ball a glancing blow. It wound up on the green about 25 feet from the hole. No suit for me. Mr. Bradley took out his four iron and lined up his shot. Last swing of the day. When his club came into contact with the ball it went screaming off the tee box but only 6 feet high. As it rocketed toward the green it was evident that it was going to go 50 yards past the hole. Then a small miracle took place. A gust of wind came out of the northeast which made the flag stand at attention. Just then the ball hit the cloth part of the flag and stopped it from going any further. It dropped on the green like a sack of rocks. The only thing we could see between the golf ball and the hole was 5" of green. We started high fiving each other like we just won the Decathlon. The three of us ran to the green like Bruce Jenner before all the surgeries and the marriage to that crazy woman with the reality TV show. Ok, it took us 3 minutes to go 188 yards, but it seemed fast. We grabbed the tape measure and the number that was going to win me the $43,000.00 suit was 7!" As we went to write the number on the marker along with my name someone earlier had hit one to 4." No suit for me. What an emotional roller coaster.

After the round on my drive home I reflected on the day's events. I had a phenomenal day and considered it a privilege to be with those members.

UNFORGETTABLE QUOTES

The following are some of the most amazing statements that I have heard over the years while on the golf course. Now keep in mind some of these statements came about because a player was under extreme distress because of their work situation, home life, or current status in the match they were playing. In any case, I think they are hysterical.

"In order for me to make this it has to go in, right?"

"From that lie, that was the greatest 8 EVER!"

"Do they make 60 degree wedges in the shape of a hybrid?"

"That was the second worse shot I have ever seen."

A player asked another player where the flag was on this particular green. "It looks like it is in the back towards the right, kind of in the front, just on the left side."

"Did that ball get to the green?" No it was short. "I guess I needed to hit it farther in order to get it there."

After hitting the drive down the fairway, "How many shots did it take me to get here?" Uh.......1.

"Is it acceptable to pee in this area?"

"I would not have to hit this ball out of the sand if it had not bounced in here!"

"How far is it to the hole from here? "142 yards." "Why is it not 150 yards?"

"I lose every time he beats me."

"I play right handed; I can't hit this shot left handed. I'm not amphibious."

"What do I have to shoot today to break 100?"

"I didn't realize golf umbrellas were used by golfers. I thought they were just for spectators."

"If I did not miss that putt I would have scored one less, right?"

"If this is called the Perfect Club, why can't I hit it on every shot?"

"Is that ball ever going to come down?"

"The less I swing the better I seem to score."

"You could have a yard sale with the amount of crap you have in this bag."

"When I take a practice swing I feel like I'm a scratch golfer."

"We have to see the ball in order to find it, right?"

"That was almost a legitimate 83."

"How do you keep track of all your shots."

"I just got a seven, what should I put on the scorecard."

Scott   Werner
was born in Baltimore Maryland. He spent the
early years of his life in the sport of powerlifting.
Scott specialized in the bench press event where
he went on to become the first man in the world
to bench press 500 lbs. in the 165 lbs. weight
class. Although Scott still stays in touch with the
fitness industry, his focus changed to the
financial industry where he
helped individuals and families with their
financial future. After a few years Scott made a
career change and moved into the golf industry
where he is currently a caddie for the Financial
Titans of the world. Scott just published his first
book "Caddy Tales" which is an exclusive behind
the scenes look at what it is like to caddie for this
unique individuals.

Printed in Great Britain
by Amazon